	DATE DUE		

Close Calls

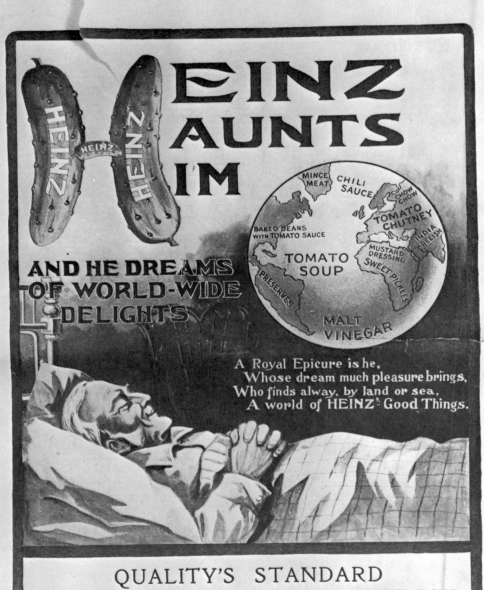

HEINZ HAUNTS HIM

AND HE DREAMS OF WORLD-WIDE DELIGHTS

MINCE MEAT · CHILI SAUCE · CHOW CHOW · TOMATO CHUTNEY · INDIA RELISH · BAKED BEANS WITH TOMATO SAUCE · MUSTARD DRESSING · SWEET PICKLES · TOMATO SOUP · PRESERVES · MALT VINEGAR

A Royal Epicure is he,
Whose dream much pleasure brings,
Who finds alway, by land or sea,
A world of HEINZ' Good Things.

QUALITY'S STANDARD

For thirty-two years we have been catering to the epicure and perfecting our 57 VARIETIES OF PURE FOOD PRODUCTS. We know what he wants and we prepare it with the utmost care.

There was a time when the housewife had to stand over the hot stove in the heated months to do her Pickling and Preserving. That day has passed. She can now secure Heinz 57 Good Things for the table, made from selected fresh fruits and vegetables, granulated sugar, and pure spices of our own grinding. Thousands of visitors each year attest to the scrupulous cleanliness and perfect equipment of our establishment. We invite your inspection when visiting Pittsburg. Courteous guides always in attendance.

OUR HANDSOME BOOKLET "THE SPICE OF LIFE," WILL GIVE YOU AN IDEA OF OUR WAY OF PERFECTLY PREPARING FOOD. SEND FOR ONE.

H. J. HEINZ CO., PITTSBURG, PA.

Close Calls

*From the Brink of Ruin
to Business Success*

By Nathan Aaseng

Lerner Publications Company
Minneapolis

To Devin

Page one: Autoworkers used 3M's Scotch masking tape to cover car parts that were not to be painted.

Page two: H.J. Heinz recognized the value of advertising his products. An early advertisement shows how Heinz effectively used pickle illustrations to develop the company's name recognition.

Library of Congress Cataloging-in-Publication Data

Aaseng, Nathan.
   Close calls: from the brink of ruin to business success / by Nathan Aaseng.
      p.   cm.
   Includes bibliographical references.
   Summary: Relates success stories of entrepreneurs such as Heinz,
Folger, Du Pont, and Chrysler, who overcame bankruptcy and other
business crises to establish thriving companies.
   ISBN 0-8225-0682-3 (lib. bdg.)
   1. Success in business—United States—Case studies—Juvenile
literature. 2. Business failures—United States—Case studies—
Juvenile literature. [1. Business enterprises. 2. Success in
business.] I. Title.
HF5386.A386   1990
650.14—dc20
                                             89-13050
                                              CIP
                                               AC

Manufactured in the United States of America

1 2 3 4 5 6 7 8 9 10 99 98 97 96 95 94 93 92 91 90

Contents

INTRODUCTION 7

BUILDING FROM THE GROUND UP—AGAIN
Du Pont 11

BANKRUPT BUT STILL IN BUSINESS
Folger's 17

BURIED BY A BUMPER CROP
Heinz 25

LOSING THE BATTLES, WINNING THE WAR
Woolworth 33

CRAZY DOW'S EXPLODING FACTORY
Dow Chemical Company 41

THE SANDPAPER THAT WOULDN'T SAND
3M 49

THE ETCH A SKETCH® SAFETY SCARE
Ohio Art Company 55

IT ALMOST WASN'T IN THE CARDS
Hallmark 61

THE AUTOMAKER'S CRISIS: DÉJÀ VU
Chrysler 67

BIBLIOGRAPHY 76

INDEX 77

After trying to run stores in several other cities, R.H. Macy found success in New York City. This store at New York City's Herald Square was billed as the world's largest.

Introduction

"HEINZ GOES BROKE!" "CHRYSLER Loses $1.1 Billion, Faces End of Road!" "Woolworth Calls It Quits!" "Fire Destroys Hallmark Warehouse!" "Du Pont Near Ruin after Blast Levels Plant!"

Unlikely headlines about some of the most successful companies in the world? Unlikely, maybe, but they are all based on fact. At one time or another, each of these large corporations faced a crisis that threatened its success.

This book is about companies and products that could easily have failed. Only the most heroic efforts and stubborn refusals to give up kept them from failing.

This book deals with two kinds of close calls. One involves an agonizing string of failures. Rowland Hussey Macy is a prime example of a bullheaded businessperson who did not quit, despite opening four stores that failed. This Massachusetts merchant launched his first store in Boston in 1844. The store went out of business soon after it opened. Undaunted, Macy quickly started a dry-goods store and struggled for two years to keep it going. That effort also ended in failure.

Macy bounced back in 1849, when he sailed to San Francisco during the California Gold Rush. He opened a general store there, supplying goods to gold prospectors. Within a year, however, the business failed and Macy returned home.

R.H. Macy

Incredibly, Macy still believed he could run a store successfully. He set up his fourth store in Haverhill, Massachusetts. It went bankrupt in 1855.

Three years later, Macy set up his fifth shop in New York City. He found that the same techniques that had failed in his other stores worked well in his New York store. Macy kept adding new lines of merchandise until his tiny shop had evolved into the United States's first department store. Annual sales from the store grew from $90,000 in 1858 to nearly $2 million in 1877, the year Macy died. By that time, Macy's store had become the largest in the world.

The stories of Heinz, Folger's, Dow, Du Pont, Chrysler, and Woolworth all tell of businesses that had to overcome continuing problems to succeed.

Another type of close call is a sudden crisis. For example, one of the most respected engineering firms, the Grumman Corporation, nearly failed before it started. In 1930 Leroy Grumman and two partners rented a garage on the south shore of Long Island, New York, to start an airplane repair business. The company's first job was to repair a wrecked seaplane.

Because only half of the plane fit through the door of the garage, Grumman workers left the nose of the plane sticking out into the street while they were working on another part of the plane. But before they could fix the plane, a motorist rammed into the part that was in the street. Since the plane was sitting where it should not have been, Grumman's company was responsible for the accident.

In order to avoid a lawsuit that the motorist threatened to file, Grumman used his equipment and mechanical knowledge to make the automobile look like new. Had the driver been seriously injured, however, the company might not have had a chance to succeed. It might never have been in a position to develop the spacecraft that landed the first human on the moon.

Hallmark, the Ohio Art Company, and 3M can all sympathize with Grumman. Each of them nearly went out of business because of a sudden crisis. Their stories are told in the following chapters.

Leroy Grumman

Eleuthère Irénée Du Pont expected that his gunpowder mills would no doubt suffer explosions. His factory consisted of several small buildings, each facing the Brandywine River. Because of the way the buildings were constructed, the force of the explosions would carry debris toward the river—away from people and other buildings.

Building From the Ground Up—Again

Du Pont

WHEN FORMER DELAWARE GOVERNOR Pete Du Pont sought the Republican party nomination for president in 1988, opponents made a point of calling him by his given name, Pierre. They wanted voters to think of the Du Ponts as an elite upper-class family that has inherited its wealth and has never had to work for a living.

It is certainly true that the Du Pont family and the massive chemical company it created are interwoven into one of the wealthiest dynasties in the world. It is also true that the Du Pont family is descended from privileged French nobility. Yet even the Du Ponts have suffered hardships. The founder of E.I. du Pont de Nemours & Co. struggled for years to keep the company in operation after a series of plant accidents.

Eleuthère Irénée Du Pont (usually called Irénée) was born in Paris, France, in 1771. His father, Pierre, had risen to a position of influence in the French government. Pierre was a skillful negotiator who helped to bring about the 1783 Treaty of Paris between the United States and Great Britain. For his efforts, he was granted a title of nobility by King Louis XVI.

Pierre soon realized that Irénée was not interested in political matters, as he was. The boy was fascinated with science, and Pierre used his political influence to get Irénée a position at the national powder works, which manufactured gunpowder.

Irénée's career in the French gunpowder mills was cut short, however, during the French Revolution. Many of the wealthiest and most influential people in France were slaughtered by the revolutionaries, and Pierre Du Pont was in grave danger. He eventually was captured and narrowly avoided execution. After he was captured and released a second time, Pierre decided to leave Paris.

In 1799 the Du Ponts—Pierre, his two sons, and their families—left for the United States. Irénée's brother Victor had already taken several trips to the United States, and Pierre was a personal friend of Thomas Jefferson, who would soon be president of the country. The Du Ponts arrived in Newport, Rhode Island, in January of 1800, after a frightful three-month ocean voyage.

When they left France, the Du Ponts were not

Irénée Du Pont

certain how they should go about starting their new lives in the United States. The answer came to Irénée one day while he was hunting. He and a friend were using American gunpowder, and their guns were misfiring about half the time. As a former trainee of the best chemists in France, Du Pont associated the problem with poor-quality gunpowder. He soon found out that high-quality gunpowder was scarce in the United States.

Irénée then visited a United States gunpowder plant, where he discovered that U.S. methods of making gunpowder were years out-of-date. It was then, in 1801, that he decided to open a gunpowder mill.

First, he had to persuade his father to finance a gunpowder manufacturing business. In the end, Pierre Du Pont agreed to provide two-thirds of the money, but Irénée had to find investors to supply the rest.

Irénée traveled to Paris to buy the equipment he needed and to find investors. He took notes on the latest methods for manufacturing gunpowder and recruited French workers for his new business. When he returned to the United States, he began searching for a suitable place to build his gunpowder mill. He finally settled on a 95-acre site on the banks of the Brandywine River near Wilmington, Delaware.

He had his mill buildings constructed with three strong walls. A weak wall and a thin, sloped roof faced the river. Thus, blasts from any accidental

A person who gives money or something else of value to a business with the expectation of getting the money back with a little extra if the business is successful is called an **investor**. Every new business requires an initial investment of some amount of money.

explosions would be directed away from the other buildings. Fewer workers would be endangered by the explosions that were bound to happen, and damage to the factory buildings would be kept to a minimum.

Construction of the buildings took longer and was more expensive than Du Pont had anticipated. Finally, in 1804, Du Pont's first gunpowder was ready for sale. The business floundered during its first 10 years, though.

Despite President Jefferson's suggestions to his military commanders that they order gunpowder from Du Pont, some officials in charge of purchasing gunpowder did not agree with Jefferson's favorable view of the French. Indifferent to the fact that Du Pont's gunpowder was obviously superior in quality and a better value, they bought as little from the new company as possible.

Instead, Du Pont relied on sales to private businesses, such as the Astor Fur Company, to keep afloat. Although sales of gunpowder were good in the company's early days, Du Pont did not make nearly enough money to keep up with the bills from creditors.

Had Irénée not been so relentless, E.I. du Pont de Nemours & Co. could have succumbed to any number of unfortunate circumstances. From out of nowhere came a false rumor that Du Pont was selling gunpowder to enemies of the United States. Irénée quickly realized that the rumor could hurt

In the 19th century, gunpowder was packed into wooden, 25-pound kegs. Du Pont also sold its gunpowder in small hunters' flasks.

An important part of the U.S. business system is the use of credit. **Credit** is the ability to get goods or services in exchange for a promise to pay later. A person who gives credit is called a **creditor**.

A company is said to make a **profit** when the money it earns from sales amounts to more than the cost of producing or buying the goods or service. Most businesses pay money to investors from the profits. Young companies generally like to use some of the profits to improve their businesses by buying better or additional equipment, building more factories, or developing new products.

A modern 25-pound gunpowder keg

his gunpowder sales in the United States, so he offered to open the company's books to anyone who wanted proof that the rumors were false. He had to fight off his father's creditors, who thought that any of the company's profits should be turned over to them.

When the company finally gained the reputation for quality that it deserved, other manufacturers began selling their own gunpowder under Du Pont's Brandywine label. Du Pont usually battled a cash shortage because many customers made no effort to pay their bills on time. He also found that some of his investors were interested only in quick profits and not in the long-term growth of the company. In order to run the company the way he wanted, Irénée bought out those investors' shares at inflated prices.

But the most devastating hardships were the plant accidents. Even Irénée's careful planning could not eliminate the risk of explosion. The refining operation was so delicate that the tiniest spark from the slightest scraping of a stone could cause an explosion. Just when the demand for gunpowder during the War of 1812 was bringing the company to profitability, the Du Pont mills were rocked by one explosion after another.

In 1815 an explosion destroyed one building and killed nine people. A fire and explosion in 1816, then a fire in 1817, caused no deaths but forced Irénée Du Pont to borrow $30,000 to rebuild the operations. While the company was reeling from these disasters, the worst catastrophe of all leveled the entire gunpowder mill complex in 1818. A disgruntled employee was blamed for starting the explosion that killed 40 people. Du Pont went deeply in debt to provide benefits for widows and orphans of employees killed in the accident, as well as to reconstruct the mill.

Du Pont continued to struggle against the odds. By his death in 1834, Du Pont had increased production to one million pounds of gunpowder per year. The company had fewer major accidents in later years and was helped by a tremendous boost in sales during the United States Civil War in the 1860s. E.I. du Pont de Nemours & Co. grew into a solid, profitable company.

New generations of Du Ponts worked out business strategies to gain a controlling interest in 54 companies and over half the United States explosives market by 1902. Since then the Du Pont businesses have expanded and begun producing a wide variety of chemicals and chemical products.

The man who saw the company through its perilous beginnings, Eleuthère Irénée Du Pont, lived just long enough to see his ponderous burden of debt reduced to a manageable load. When he died, he was on a trip to meet with creditors about the remainder of the company's debts.

Debt is an obligation to pay something, like a bill. Companies or individuals go into **bankruptcy** when they cannot pay their debts within a reasonable amount of time.

Stocks are small parts of ownership in a company. Ownership is usually divided among many shareholders, or owners. When a person owns stock in a business, he or she is said to have an interest in the business. A person who owns most of the stocks in a business has a **controlling interest**.

Du Pont gradually became known for making products other than gunpowder, such as fabric that protects its wearers from burns.

Bankrupt but Still in Business

Folger's

James Folger

FOR MOST BUSINESSPEOPLE, BANKRUPTcy signals the end of their business dreams. But when James Folger went bankrupt, he scarcely seemed to notice. His was a world in which failure was not uncommon and where security was temporary. In the midst of a financial disaster, Folger kept operating his business as if nothing had happened. After 10 years, he finally paid off the last of the money he owed.

James Folger was born in 1835 on the island of Nantucket, off the coast of Massachusetts. Nantucket was a large whaling community, a bustling town of 10,000 people. Folger's father, Samuel, had worked his way up from blacksmith to head of a large construction shop and owner of 2 of the 90 ships in town.

Nearly everything that the people of Nantucket had worked for, however, went up in smoke on July 13, 1846. A fire started in the business district and raged through the town for an entire day. By the time firefighters brought it under control, the fire had destroyed 33 acres of buildings and property, including Samuel Folger's shop and his two ships. Jim Folger was 11 at the time. The fire indirectly led Folger into the business that made his name a household word.

No sooner had the devastating fire been put out than the townspeople started ferrying wood, bricks, and other building materials from the mainland. They quickly began rebuilding the town.

While working with his older brothers on the reconstruction, Jim learned carpentry skills, which turned out to be useful when it became obvious that whales were growing too scarce for whaling to restore the town's economy. Despite the efforts of its citizens, Nantucket never regained its wealth.

Like many of the island's families, the Folgers decided to send some of their sons to California. There, it was said, the hills were practically bursting with gold. Although he was only 14 years old, Jim Folger was judged to be good enough with his hands to support himself, and he went to California with two older brothers in the fall of 1849.

The Folgers arrived in San Francisco the next spring, at the peak of the gold rush. The city, which was a base for gold prospectors, grew from 800

Jim Folger began working for William Bovee at Pioneer Steam Coffee and Spice Mills. Folger later bought the business.

A basic rule of business involves supply and demand. The amount or number of a product, in this case carpentry labor, offered for sale (at different prices) at any certain time is called **supply. Demand** is the amount or number of products that people are willing to buy (at different prices) at any certain time. In general, the greater the demand for a product, the higher the price can be set.

The **market** for coffee or any other product or service means the potential buyers for that product.

residents to 40,000 in just two years. Carpenters were in great demand and could get top wages. For that reason, Jim stayed behind to work in San Francisco while his brothers went in search of gold.

Folger's first employer was William Bovee, who had sold his coffee-roasting business in New York City to seek his fortune in the gold fields. Unable to find gold, Bovee decided to return to his old business, selling coffee and spices. He hired Jim Folger to help him build a spice and coffee mill.

The business, Pioneer Steam Coffee and Spice Mills, found a growing market in California. People were tired of roasting their own green coffee beans. Bovee had even greater success when he saved the miners one more step by grinding the coffee before he sold it.

Shortly after it was opened, the coffee mill received an order so large that Bovee could not possibly fill it in time by using hand-cranked roasting drums. With Folger's help, he constructed a windmill using sails from ships. Unfortunately, the windmill was completed just as the summer winds died out. It stood idle during the calm weather, and Bovee lost his contract. He then imported a steam engine to boost his production.

After a year of working for Bovee, Jim Folger headed into the California hills loaded with a trunk full of coffee and some gold-panning equipment. Not only did he find a small deposit of gold, he also found that the miners liked the coffee he sold. He used his gold findings to set up his own store in the middle of mining country. Despite his youth and inexperience, the 16-year-old Folger knew how to handle himself. After doing brisk business for two years, he sold the store for a tidy profit and returned to San Francisco.

Eventually, he found himself back with Bovee, working primarily as a traveling salesman. His success in selling to customers in the gold fields triggered a boycott of Pioneer coffee by jealous coffee distributors. The Pioneer coffee was so well-liked, however, that customers refused to accept other coffee.

In 1859 Bovee returned to the gold fields. He sold most of his interest in the coffee mill to Folger and a partner. During prosperous times in the early

A **contract** is a business agreement in which one person or business agrees to supply another person or business with a certain amount of goods and services at a fixed price and by a certain time.

The word **production** refers to all activities involved in converting natural resources, such as coffee beans, into finished goods, such as ground and roasted coffee. The word **manufacturing** refers to the making of articles by hand or with machines.

A **boycott** is an effort to persuade large numbers of people not to buy or use certain products. People who organize boycotts hope a company will be hurt by lost sales.

Getting coffee from one place to another is called **distribution**. The product may go directly from the manufacturer to the consumer, or it may go from the manufacturer to a **distributor** (frequently a store) and then to the consumer.

A collection of coffee cans used by Folger's company in its early days

1860s, Marden & Folger, as the company was then called, borrowed money to enlarge its facilities. During the economic chaos that followed the Civil War, coffee sales fell so drastically that Marden & Folger could not begin to pay its debts. The company was forced to declare bankruptcy in 1865.

Bankruptcy should have brought an end to Folger's business pursuits. But in the loose atmosphere of the sprawling frontier town, ordinary business rules were ignored. Not only did Folger keep going, but he went further into debt to buy out his partner. He renamed the company J.A. Folger & Co. Folger's creditors thought they would be more likely to get their money back if Folger kept running the business than if they tried to run it themselves. Thus, the coffee and spice miller was given some time to make his business profitable.

Perhaps Folger's creditors would not have been as understanding if they had known it would take Folger 10 years to repay the debts. But Folger stubbornly kept at his task, finding the best blend of coffees, obtaining the finest spices, and selling to customers all over California. Along with a reputation for quality, Folger earned a reputation for honesty. In 1874, he paid the last of his debts. J.A. Folger & Co. was in the clear.

Having weathered the economic crisis, Folger focused on expansion. He sent salespeople into the lumber and mining towns of the Northwest and down the California coast nearly to Mexico. The

For a time, Folger sold coffee under the brand name of Golden Gate. Golden Gate is the name of a channel of water between San Francisco and land to the north of the city.

Many companies realize the value of **expanding** (becoming bigger or developing different aspects of the business). Often, by expanding, a company can offer its customers more or better service.

company continued to expand, moving into larger facilities five times within 50 years.

By the time of Folger's death in 1889, settlers throughout the entire western United States were not content with just any coffee and spices; they wanted Folger's coffee and spices. Continued expansion by James Folger's children turned Folger's coffee and its offshoot, Schilling spices, into popular national brands. James Folger had made the most of a second chance that few businesspeople receive.

H.J. Heinz, known for treating his employees well, visited with farm workers from a horse-drawn wagon.

Buried by a Bumper Crop

Heinz

H.J. HEINZ IS THE NAME THAT MAKES people think of ketchup. But there was a time when the name made grocers, produce farmers, and other creditors think about the money Heinz owed them. Despite his keen sales talent, Harry Heinz got himself into a bind that few people could have overcome. It took every scrap of his energy, creativity, and marketing genius to win back his place as a supplier of canned and bottled foods.

Henry John Heinz, called Harry by his family, was born in Pittsburgh, Pennsylvania, in 1844. The family moved to Sharpsburg, six miles outside Pittsburgh, when Harry was five years old. His father ran a construction and brick-making business. His mother raised vegetables in a four-acre garden behind the house.

At the age of eight, Harry began selling excess vegetables from his mother's garden to neighbors. He was so successful that within two years he had graduated from carrying the produce in baskets to pushing it in wheelbarrows. By the age of 12, he had outgrown the wheelbarrow and instead used a horse and cart. Still not content with the size of the operation, he used hotbeds and increased fertilization to triple the garden's production. At the age of 15, he was selling so much produce to local grocers that he hired his brothers and sisters and some neighborhood children to help him keep up with the demand. He began bottling horseradish and selling that to local merchants as well. Heinz bottled the horseradish in clear jars instead of the usual green or brown glass so customers could see its quality.

Harry also became more involved in his father's brick business. He took some college business courses and then did the bookkeeping for his father. When he was 21, he used his savings to buy a half interest in the business.

As a new partner, Harry wasted no time in implementing new ideas. He installed a heating and drying system in the brick plant, which made it possible for the factory to manufacture bricks all year long instead of only in warm weather.

Harry had barely scratched the surface, however. A few years later, when his father returned from a long trip to Europe, he had a surprise waiting for

The way a product is packaged can influence sales. The **packaging** for Heinz's horseradish was a clear jar, so customers could see the product. At that time, most bottled horseradish was packaged in brown or green glass jars and sometimes contained additional ingredients like turnips, leaves, and wood fiber that many customers did not like. Because Heinz packaged his horseradish in clear jars, customers could see that it did not contain the offensive ingredients. Buyers are also influenced simply by a product's appearance. If two items are exactly alike and their prices are the same, customers probably will buy the product that has a package that they like.

him. Harry had built a new home for his parents. He had used bricks from his father's business and had paid the other construction costs by collecting unpaid bills from customers. His father had long since given up on collecting the debts.

When he was 25, in 1869, Harry teamed up with a friend, L.C. Noble, to form a horseradish and pickle-packing company. That was the same year that Harry married Sarah (Sallie) Sloan Young. Sallie gave birth to a daughter two years later, and the couple had three more children, sons, in following years. Heinz and Noble quickly became successful, selling products under the name Anchor Brand. Three years after they had started the company, the two took in a new partner, E.J. Noble, the brother of L.C. Noble. The company was renamed Heinz, Noble & Company.

H.J. Heinz as a young man

Up to that time, everything had come quite easily for the young company. However, Heinz, Noble & Company soon faced financial troubles. The partners had borrowed heavily to expand the business. By 1875 it occupied a large office and storeroom in Pittsburgh and was producing vinegar, sauerkraut, and celery sauce, in addition to pickles and horseradish. Heinz was selling the products in style, having his salespeople make their rounds in expensive wagons drawn by some of the company's 25 beautiful horses.

In anticipation of more profits, Heinz, Noble & Company signed contracts with several large produce farms in 1874 to buy, at an agreed price, all the cucumbers and cabbage the farms grew. The company's problems began when 1874 turned out to be a spectacular year for farming. With a bumper crop of vegetables flooding the market, the price for cucumbers and cabbage dropped greatly. Heinz was stuck with far more produce than he could use at a price far greater than it was worth.

While Heinz, Noble & Company was dealing with its own financial disaster, a business panic was affecting all the banks in the area. Heinz was unable to borrow money from the banks to see him through the bad year. He tried to save the business by borrowing from friends, from his life insurance policy, and against the equity on his house and the one he had built for his parents. But even that amount was too little to bail out the business for more than a few months.

Heinz was twice arrested on charges of fraud. Although he cleared himself of any wrongdoing, his reputation was shattered. Everything he had, plus his friends' money and his parents' house, was lost when Heinz, Noble & Company declared bankruptcy in 1875.

Considered a bad risk by banks that refused to lend money to him, Heinz did not seem to have much of a future in business. Store owners with whom he had dealt for years would not even give him credit to buy groceries to feed his family.

Heinz again turned to relatives for help. He was convinced that he had been on the right track and

Usually, when people buy houses, they make a small payment toward the total cost, then make monthly payments on a mortgage, or loan, for the remainder. Part of each payment goes toward a fee for borrowing the money, while the rest goes toward the cost of the house. The total amount that the buyers have paid toward the cost of the house represents their **equity**; it's the amount of money they will have left if they sell the house and pay off the remainder of the mortgage.

that there was an untapped consumer demand for ready-made food products. He saw that people were growing tired of routine, uninteresting meals and were looking for items such as vinegar, pickles, and horseradish to add some zest. Yet they didn't like to prepare these foods because of the work involved. Crushing horseradish usually made a person's eyes sting. Someone willing to prepare those food items would certainly find buyers. Having learned from his mistakes, all Heinz needed was another chance. Since the terms of his bankruptcy prohibited him from owning shares in a business, he also needed someone willing to head up the venture.

In 1876 Heinz persuaded a cousin, Frank, and a

Heinz's second business venture eventually grew large enough to warrant a large manufacturing complex.

brother, John, to start a food-processing company and hire him as the manager. One of F & J Heinz Company's most profitable products was tomato ketchup. Ketchup took an entire day to make in the home. Heinz's recipe of tomatoes, sugar, salt, onions, spices, and flavorings was available on grocery store shelves in long-necked bottles.

Because the new company was under-capitalized, Heinz had to watch pennies carefully. It took some humility for Heinz to run the business on a shoestring budget. Instead of a stylish buggy and a team of matching horses, he made do with a small cart and one blind horse.

Gradually Heinz won back the trust of Pittsburgh-area creditors. He was discharged from bankruptcy and made enough money as manager eventually to buy a portion of his cousin's interest in the business. Although he was not required by law to pay back any of the money his former business owed, Heinz was determined to pay back his share of the debts. It took him until 1888 to pay the last creditor. He then bought his brother's share of the company and renamed it the H.J. Heinz Company.

Heinz's biggest breakthrough came at the Columbian Exposition in Chicago. For a while it seemed that this fair, honoring the 400th anniversary of Christopher Columbus's voyage, wasn't going to happen. Organization problems delayed the opening until 1893. Heinz had hoped to use a booth to advertise and give away samples of his products. To

This type of bottle was used for Heinz ketchup from 1889 to 1910.

If a company is said to be **under-capitalized**, it means that the company has too little money to operate efficiently.

This ketchup bottle, used (along with other shapes) by Heinz from 1890 to 1900, was the forerunner of Heinz's familiar octagon-shaped bottle.

Advertising is the presentation of ideas, goods, and services to the public; it is paid for by a sponsor. **Promotion** is all of a company's selling activities, including advertising, face-to-face selling, and special efforts such as coupons or give-aways.

his disappointment, he was assigned a booth on the second floor of an agriculture building. People usually looked over the displays on the first floor, then left the building without venturing upstairs.

Realizing he could not attract many passersby from the location, Heinz hired boys to pass out cards that could be exchanged for free gifts at the Heinz booth. Thousands of curious people sought out the Heinz booth to get something for nothing. So many flocked to his exhibit, in fact, that police had to limit the traffic until new supports could added to hold up the second floor of the building. Heinz's giveaway was a pickle charm souvenir, which was an excellent advertising gimmick to put the Heinz name before the public.

One day Heinz saw an advertisement for "21 styles of shoes." He thought it was an eye-catching slogan and he thought about ways he could use something similar to promote his food products. For some reason he liked the sound of "57" and began to use that in his slogan, even though the company made more than 57 different products. From that day on, Heinz promoted "57 varieties."

Heinz created more attention-drawing spectacles. He leased an entire pier that jutted into the ocean off Atlantic City, New Jersey, and set up a tourist center to give away samples of Heinz products. One of the attractions of the pier was a museum of Heinz's art collection. In 1900 Heinz erected New York City's first large electric sign. It used 1,200 light

bulbs and had a 40-foot-long pickle. Retaining his fondness for elegant transportation, Heinz bought a fleet of white wagons. The wagons were pulled by black horses from the company's stable. Heinz was also one of the first business owners to open his factories for public tours.

Whether it was his gimmicks, the quality of his products, the generous way he treated employees, or a combination of the three, Heinz became a familiar name in the food business. Heinz labels were recognized not only on grocery shelves but in restaurants throughout the United States. Working his way out of a terrible situation, H.J. Heinz created a company that, more than 70 years after his death, produced 3,000 products and employed more than 45,000 people.

This large advertisement on the side of a New York City building was one of several ways Heinz advertised its products to the public.

Losing the Battles, Winning the War

Woolworth

Frank Winfield Woolworth was not a promising store clerk. He was refused employment at several stores because he didn't know the business. When he finally did land a job, he made frequent mistakes. At his second job, Woolworth's salary was cut 20 percent because he was such a poor salesperson. Finally, Woolworth ran his own store less than four months before it failed.

All of the failures and shortcomings should have told him that he was better off working on his parents' farm. But Frank had disliked farming from an early age, so much that he had often dreamed about escaping the farm. After losing almost all the battles along the way, Woolworth eventually won the war.

Frank Woolworth was born in Rodman, New York, in 1852. As a young boy his favorite game was "playing store," and it was a fascination that he never outgrew. He began working full time on the family's 108-acre farm at the age of 16, immediately after finishing his schooling. But he considered the work to be sheer drudgery, and he took a business course at a local college to prepare himself for a different career.

Woolworth was 21 years old before he found a store owner willing to take a chance on hiring him. Even then he had to work three months without pay to gain experience for a paying job. The owners of Augsbury & Moore Corner Store, in Watertown, New York, then put him on a six-day, 84-hour work week and paid him less than 4½ cents per hour.

For several months, Woolworth exasperated his employers because he knew so little about the store. He was once sent home because he had forgotten to put on a proper white shirt.

After a couple of years with Augsbury & Moore, Woolworth took a new job with A. Bushnell & Company. The owners of this dry-goods and carpet store were even less impressed with his talents than his first employer had been at first. Woolworth's salary was cut from $10 to $8 per week because of his poor sales record. Woolworth worked much harder and longer to prove he could do the job well. The only result, however, was that he collapsed of exhaustion, lost his job, and spent half a year recovering his health. Woolworth married Jennie Creighton, a seamstress who had helped nurse

Woolworth got his start at the Augsbury & Moore Corner Store in Watertown, New York, in 1873. Years later, when William Moore retired, Woolworth added the store to his fast-growing chain of five-and-ten stores.

him back to health. The couple eventually had three daughters.

Woolworth's sympathetic former employer, William Moore, offered him his old job at Augsbury & Moore, which had become Moore & Smith's Corner Store. It was there that Frank Woolworth showed a talent for window displays. He was soon to get his largest break. In 1878 Moore was faced with a growing stack of unpaid bills as well as too much merchandise, and he needed to sell some excess goods. He had Woolworth set up a new type of display. The "five-cent counter" had worked well in some Midwestern stores. Woolworth laid out a table full of pins, combs, pencils, soap, and other small items. Over the display, he posted a sign to inform customers that anything on the table could be bought for five cents.

While Moore didn't really expect to make a great deal of money off such low-priced merchandise, the five-cent table would at least attract customers to the store. Once they were inside the store, they might buy some of the higher-priced items. Woolworth took great care in arranging and restocking the table, and customers snatched up the bargains. The counter was so popular that Woolworth began to think about a giant version of the five-cent table. He thought he could make money with an entire store stocked entirely with these inexpensive little notions.

Woolworth was fortunate to have an employer who was willing to help. While Woolworth scouted locations for a new store in 1879, Moore backed him with a $315 loan of merchandise in order to get the young man started. Woolworth selected Utica, New York, in which to open his first store. Business started off briskly in his "Great 5-cent Store." The night before the store was to open, a woman interrupted Woolworth's frantic organizing efforts to buy a coal shovel from him. Woolworth sold $244.44 in merchandise during the first week. The store, however, was a tiny cubicle that was too far away from the town's main businesses to attract many customers. Interest in the new store began to subside, and Woolworth decided to close up shop while he was $250 ahead. His great business venture had lasted less than four months.

Woolworth took the business failure in stride. He was convinced the five-cent store was a good idea. Instead of bemoaning his failure, he simply vowed to do better next time.

Merchants can usually maintain their profits by buying and selling in large quantities. Generally, merchants who buy large amounts of goods from a manufacturer will receive a discount on the price for each item. The merchants can then pass those savings on to customers, who are more likely to buy from a store that offers a lower price. While the merchants may make a smaller amount of profit on each item, they make more money in the end because they have sold much more merchandise than they would have at the higher price.

Woolworth's store in Lancaster, Pennsylvania, was an instant success with its low-priced merchandise.

A month later, on the advice of a friend, he opened a store in Lancaster, Pennsylvania. Cleaning out a shabby, abandoned store, he began arranging his merchandise into an attractive display.

Opening day brought with it a feeling of doom. Woolworth opened the store on the day the circus was in town. After nervously tending an empty store all day, Woolworth was suddenly swamped with customers returning from the circus parade. Within a few hours, he had sold nearly a third of his

Woolworth stores emphasized prices in their product displays.

stock. At this store, with its fine location, the rush continued. Woolworth sold out his entire stock three times within three weeks. Soon his greatest worry was finding enough merchandise to keep his store full. A year after opening the Lancaster store, Woolworth expanded his line of goods by introducing 10-cent merchandise to go along with his 5-cent items. The shop soon became known as the five-and-ten store.

Woolworth, however, had not had his last failure. Flushed with success, he tried to expand his ventures into a chain of stores. Before long he had five-and-ten stores operating in the Pennsylvania towns of Harrisburg and York. Both failed, as did a brief experiment in adding a 25-cent counter.

It would have been practical for Woolworth to live on the earnings from his one successful store. After all, by 1882 his nickel and dime items were bringing in more than $24,000 a year. But Woolworth was committed to the idea of a chain of stores. He thought the key to success in selling inexpensive items was to buy and sell in huge quantities. In order to sell large amounts of goods, Woolworth felt he needed dozens of stores.

Woolworth found partners willing to invest in and manage new stores. By 1886 there were seven Woolworth stores in Pennsylvania, New Jersey, and New York. From 1888 on, Woolworth had enough money to open new stores without partners. Instead, he hired managers to run the stores for him.

Woolworth continued to run his growing empire by doing almost everything by himself. He arranged all the store displays, bought the merchandise, and offered daily advice to the managers. When he spent two months in bed with typhoid fever toward the end of 1888, he discovered that others could handle many of his tasks quite well. He began to assign those tasks to assistants to free himself for other, more ambitious projects. The Woolworth empire grew ever larger. Woolworth expanded into England in 1909, and three years later he merged with five of his rivals—longtime friends who operated five-and-ten stores in other markets.

Frank Woolworth

Woolworth stores held fast to the founder's policy of selling nothing in the store for more than a dime until long after his death in 1919. By that time the company was an established force in the retail market. Those who had watched Frank Woolworth fumble his way from one disaster to the next in his early years must have looked on in disbelief. Who else but Frank Woolworth could lose so many battles and still come out on top?

Crazy Dow's Exploding Factory

Dow Chemical Company

Herbert Dow

IN THE 1890s, MOST RESIDENTS OF Midland, Michigan, would not have believed the Dow Chemical Company would ever be successful. There was no hint that the company would one day do more than $11 billion worth of business in a single year.

Herbert Henry Dow was not nicknamed Crazy Dow for no reason. He was a man trying to make a living by mining salt water in the middle of Michigan. No one knew exactly what Dow was doing, but he certainly was not making any money. Even when he wasn't rebuilding from plant explosions, Dow's company was unprofitable.

While setting up his business, Dow faced many discouraging obstacles. He had little money, few management skills, and partners who thwarted him

41

at every step. Processes he used failed to work as expected, vats exploded for no apparent reason, and powerful foreign competitors started price wars. All of these problems, along with a business panic, hindered Crazy Dow's efforts to build a money-making business. Yet somehow Dow survived the disastrous beginning and built his company into a successful member of the chemical industry.

Herbert Dow was born in Belleville, Ontario, in 1866, and grew up in Cleveland, Ohio. His father was a skilled and creative mechanic, and Herbert inherited the same talents. In his mid-teens, Herbert read about a crude incubator that an Australian had invented for hatching ostrich eggs. Dow thought he could use the same idea to hatch chicken eggs. After 39 failed attempts to make an incubator that could hold a constant temperature, Dow finally succeeded. Before Dow could make much money from the idea, however, some of his first customers copied his plans and began manufacturing their own incubators.

Dow wanted to be an architect, but he did not have money for college. When he was offered a scholarship by the Case School of Applied Sciences in Cleveland, he accepted it even though the school did not offer classes in architecture.

During his senior year, Dow needed some natural gas for a research project. He knew that natural gas came out of the ground along with the brine, or saltwater, that processors collected to refine into

Competition is one of the basic features of the U.S. business system. **Competition** means trying to get something that others are also trying to get. Competition in business can occur in many ways. Producers compete with each other for the most customers. Companies compete to make the best-quality or lowest-priced product or service. Sometimes competitors engage in **price wars**, keeping prices below a normal profit-making level in an effort to win customers away from other businesses and weaken the competition's financial position.

Brine wells like this one provided the liquid that Dow refined to produce bromine and chlorine.

In a process called **research and development**, many companies conduct experiments to create new products or improve existing products. **Research** is investigation aimed at discovering new scientific knowledge. **Development** is the attempt to use new knowledge to make useful products or processes.

salt. Dow traveled to a nearby brine well to get a small amount of natural gas. While collecting his sample, he was given a taste of the brine that was being pumped out of the earth. Instead of simply being salty, the liquid was extremely bitter tasting. Out of curiosity, Dow analyzed the brine to see what made it so bitter. He found out that it contained a high level of bromine, an expensive chemical used in medicines and film developing.

In 1888 Dow worked as a chemistry teacher, but he frequently thought about the brine sample. He knew there would be a good market for bromine if he could find a cheap way to produce it. Other methods used massive amounts of fuel to heat the brine until the bromine separated from the rest of the mixture. Dow eventually came up with the idea of using chemicals and forced air to extract the bromine.

On the basis of a few laboratory experiments, the 23-year-old Dow talked some Ohio merchants into investing in his new venture. Renting a shed in Canton, Ohio, Dow began the Canton Chemical Company in 1889. His process did produce bromine, but in such small quantities and at such expense that he went out of business in less than a year.

Dow's experience with the egg incubator had taught him the value of persistence, however. Rather than quitting, Dow kept trying to perfect his process. He was eager to try out a new method that would use electricity to pull the bromine out of

Herbert Dow set up his second business in a grain mill.
The tower next to the mill building housed a brine well.

brine. He knew that bromine-rich brine could be found in Midland, Michigan, so he established a new plant there. Dow persuaded a family friend to invest $375 in his new project. In August 1890, he rented an idle brine well and a grain mill, and set up the Midland Chemical Company.

Even though Dow proved that his revolutionary

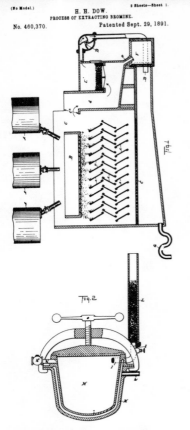

Fig.1

Fig.2

Drawings from Dow's patent application for a new way of separating bromine from brine

A **patent** is the exclusive right to own, use, and dispose of an invention. The U.S. Patent Office issues more than 1,200 patents each week. Patents for inventions are granted to the owner for 17 years; then the patent expires and the patent owner no longer has exclusive rights to the invention.

method would work, this venture seemed headed for failure. As before, Dow worked 18-hour days and used cheap, inferior equipment. His scientific dabblings earned him nothing but the nickname "Crazy Dow" from Midland's residents. Dow found more financial backers to keep his business from going bankrupt, but they quickly grew weary of Dow's requests for more money. By the summer of 1892, they refused to give him more money. Dow's second business failed.

Dow, however, remained convinced that his scientific process would work if he could somehow manage the financial end of the business better. He again persuaded a group of businesspeople to back a new business. This time it was not a nickel-and-dime collection of small investors, but a wealthy group of Cleveland businesspeople, led by B.E. Helman. Dow had thousands of dollars with which to build a modern plant with powerful electrical equipment. However, he and Helman, who considered himself Dow's boss, fought often. Dow continued to work feverishly. He and his wife often slept on cots in the factory boiler room so that Dow's work would not be interrupted. New problems always came up, though.

Finally, in 1893, just when the company began to make money, Helman demoted Dow and hired someone else to take over as general manager of the company. Dow had little choice but to keep working for Helman, since he had sold his patents for the separating process to the company.

During this discouraging time, Dow experimented with methods of extracting chlorine from brine. Both industry and individual consumers had found a variety of uses for chlorine. After determining that there was nearly 100 times more chlorine than bromine in the brine, Dow set out to find a way to separate the chlorine from the rest of the liquid.

Two months after the Midland Chemical Company's directors gave Dow permission to go ahead with his plans, an explosion ripped through the new chlorine-manufacturing plant. The resulting fire nearly destroyed the bromine-production facilities as well. Shaken by this close call, the directors ordered Dow to stop work on chlorine production. That was the last straw for the 29-year-old inventor, who left the company. Most Midland residents thought they had seen the last of Crazy Dow.

But in 1895, Dow again persuaded people—old professors and acquaintances from the Case School of Applied Sciences—to invest in a new project. He set up the Dow Process Company in Navarre, Ohio. One resident of the town was so frightened by Dow's strange plant that he offered Dow $1,000 to leave the community. Six months later, Dow did leave, to the anguish of his backers. They thought Dow was being awfully loose with their money, because he had plans to build a huge chlorine plant in Midland again.

As he had always done when his investors balked, Dow simply recruited new backers. In May of 1897, he started the Dow Chemical Company. By this time, the bromine-separating process that he had sold had been proven to work, and Dow's new-found credibility allowed him to attract more investors. To the astonishment of Midland residents, Crazy Dow began constructing an enormous chlorine complex. He still rode his bicycle to work every day, and yet, he was spending money as if he were a wealthy oil baron.

Dow still had flaws to work out of his chlorine process. The plant did not produce even half of its nine-ton capacity at the best of times, and mechanical breakdowns frequently stopped production altogether. Dangerous explosions rocked the plant again and again. For some mysterious reason, the electrical cells that were the key to the separation process kept blowing up. Finally, the company sold its first chlorine bleach the next year. Then the British chlorine industry leaders cut their prices in half in an effort to drive new United States companies out of business.

Dow's investors were getting nervous. Dow stalled for time, believing he was on the verge of the breakthrough that would make them all rich. But he knew that he had to figure out why the electric cells kept exploding.

Dow's brother-in-law, Tom Griswold, finally discovered the problem. A flaw in the equipment allowed a gas substance to mix with the chlorine. The mixture caused the violent reaction. Griswold

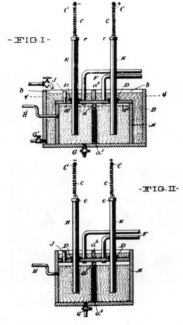

Drawings from Dow's patent application for an electrolytic cell that he used to remove chlorine from brine

easily solved the problem. Dow's problems weren't over yet, though. Powerful German chemical companies, angry with Dow for invading European markets with his products, staged an all-out price war. They put tons of their products on the United States market at a price that was far less than their production costs. Although they would lose money in the short run, they thought they could force Dow out of business, and that would help them in the long run.

Dow responded by buying the German product at the low price in the United States and selling it for a profit in Europe. Once the Germans realized what he was doing, they quickly called for a truce.

Herbert Dow faced one final barrier—a business panic in 1907. After his initial success in the business, Dow had continued to expand his operations. Some of his investments had failed miserably, however. When a bank failure sent the business community into a depression, Dow was hit hard. Although no one knew it at the time, Dow Chemical Company was broke. Before anyone noticed there was no money, Dow had already weathered the financial storm. By 1910 business was again on the upswing.

With its emphasis on research and innovation, Dow Chemical Company eventually grew into one of the largest chemical companies in the world. After four tries and 20 years, Herbert Dow had proved that he was not crazy after all.

Dow Chemical Company eventually began developing even more products for the home, including Handi-Wrap, a clear plastic used mainly for wrapping food.

The Sandpaper That Wouldn't Sand

3M

Minnesota Mining and Manufacturing, or 3M, began as a mining venture. Its founders took corundum from a mine site near Crystal Bay, Minnesota. When the mining end of the business failed, the company looked for other ways to make money.

THERE IS A SIMPLE EXPLANATION FOR the name 3M. It is a logical shortening of the company's original name, "*M*innesota *M*ining and *M*anufacturing." However, there is no simple explanation for why "mining" is part of that title. 3M is a Minnesota-based company known for its products, including Scotch brand tapes, Scotchgard fabric protector, adhesives, abrasives, reflective coatings, building materials, and film. Where's the mining?

The company was originally formed to mine a mineral that investors thought would be worth a fortune. Instead, the mineral turned out to be worthless. Somehow, despite losing its very reason for being, 3M beat the odds to become an extremely successful corporation.

The 3M company can trace its beginnings to the

discovery of a mineral thought to be corundum near the shores of Lake Superior, not far from Two Harbors, Minnesota, in 1902. Corundum is considered to be the second-hardest pure mineral in the world, after diamonds. It was needed for sanding and sharpening products, such as grinding wheels. A group of businessmen from Two Harbors formed a company to mine the material. The group included a doctor, a lawyer, a butcher, and two railroad men, none of whom had mining experience. The company was called Minnesota Mining and Manufacturing, with the emphasis on mining.

The company's founders might have suspected that the rosy predictions about the mineral's wealth were somewhat exaggerated when a business that had beaten them to the mines went bankrupt. But they went ahead and by 1904 had processed one ton of material. The quick sale of this amount of material supported a feeling among the directors that they were sitting on a fortune. With 2½ more tons quickly readied for sale, they celebrated the bright future by voting themselves hefty salaries.

But months passed without another sale. Salaries were eliminated, but debts still mounted. The company tried to find new investors, but no one would buy Minnesota Mining and Manufacturing stock at any price.

Finally, in 1905 two St. Paul men came to the rescue. Edgar Ober talked his wealthy friend, Lucius Ordway, into joining him in buying the company.

A company's **board of directors** is elected by **stockholders**, or people who own shares in the corporation, and is the company's highest power. The board of directors usually votes on important decisions for the company.

Edgar Ober

Lucius Ordway

They believed that they could clear the company's debts and set up a profitable operation with about $40,000. The plan was to break into the existing markets by selling sandpaper made with imported garnet, a mineral commonly used as an abrasive then. When the company's reputation was established in the market, it would introduce the corundum.

Ober and Ordway's cost estimates were wrong. Ordway had to invest $100,000 before the company was able to get its product back in circulation. As sales lagged far behind expenses in 1906, the investment grew to more than $200,000.

In 1907 Ordway discovered that all that money might have been spent for nothing. After the material had been mined for more than five years, the partners finally found out that the corundum from Two Harbors was of such poor quality that it was worthless as an abrasive. The mine, which had been a risky venture even in the best of times, now had nothing of value to offer.

Instead of cutting their losses and dissolving the business, Ordway and Ober stubbornly pressed ahead. They continued to manufacture sandpaper from imported materials. Their problems continued to mount, however. The company's poorly-paid salespeople frequently quit. After moving the operation to Duluth, Minnesota, they found that humidity along Lake Superior was too high to allow for efficient drying of the sandpaper after abrasive materials were glued to the paper backing. The company was moved to St. Paul, Minnesota, in 1910. Shortly after 3M moved into its newly constructed plant, a floor collapsed from the weight of 100-pound sacks of abrasives. Worst of all, Minnesota Mining and Manufacturing had an inferior product and everyone knew it.

An energetic 24-year-old bookkeeper finally helped the company out of its maze of failure. For lack of anyone more qualified, William McKnight was named 3M's national sales manager. In an effort to pinpoint the company's problems, McKnight went straight to the workers who were using his company's products. Under his leadership, quality-control problems and customer complaints were identified and resolved. By 1914 the company was gradually selling more and more sandpaper and had actually begun to make money.

William McKnight with his daughter, Virginia

But disaster struck again. Suddenly even 3M's best customers shipped back large amounts of sandpaper and refused to buy more. For some unknown reason, the sandpaper had become unusable: The garnet fell from the paper as soon as workers began using it. While the rejects came pouring back, the company tried to figure out why the sandpaper had gone bad.

Several weeks later, a worker noticed an oily film on water in a pail. There was some crushed garnet in the bottom of the pail. If the garnet somehow contained oil, that would explain why it was not staying glued to the paper.

Controlling the quality of a product is crucial to a business's success. Good quality depends on the product's design, whether the equipment used to make it is up-to-date and well-maintained, and the people doing the job. **Quality control** refers to the methods used to assure that a product consistently meets the desired level of quality. McKnight set up a small department to oversee the company's quality control efforts.

3M's "wetordry" sandpaper was a new product that the company obtained by chance.

An investigation found that the garnet was indeed contaminated by oil. It had been shipped from Spain on a vessel that was also carrying olive oil. The ship had run into a violent storm at sea, and some of the casks holding the oil had split open. The oil leaked into bags of garnet.

With this mystery finally solved, Minnesota Mining and Manufacturing again went about the painfully slow process of regaining the trust of its customers. McKnight also set up a quality control unit to ensure that no such problem developed again. The laboratory and an emphasis on technology helped the company make discoveries that led to new products and growing profits.

About this time, the automobile industry was looking for new types of abrasives that could speed up its production. After months of research, 3M developed a sandpaper made with aluminum oxide, an artificial mineral. This new paper quickly impressed customers as the best sandpaper available for metalworking. With help from orders for the new product, the company doubled its total sales in two years.

When a man, looking to eliminate the dust problems created by sanding, thought of a sandpaper that could work even when wet, 3M picked up on the idea. The company's line of wet-or-dry sandpaper, introduced in 1921, established 3M as the leader in the field.

When the automotive industry began offering

two-tone paint on cars, it provided another opportunity for 3M. Although customers liked this innovation, automobile painters hated it. In order to keep the colors separate, they had to use glue or surgical tape to keep newspapers over the portions that they didn't want to paint. Unfortunately, those adhesive products frequently caused more problems. In 1925 3M invented masking tape, which held newspapers in place and still pulled off easily without damaging the paint.

An early complaint about the sticking ability of the masking tape is credited with inspiring 3M's brand name "Scotch." An angry customer reportedly told a salesman, "Take this tape back to your stingy Scotch bosses and tell them to put more adhesive on it."

In 1930, after exhaustive research, the company perfected a transparent cellophane tape that was used to seal packages. Customers soon found other uses for the tape—repairing torn paper and fastening things together.

3M continued to develop new products in more than 40 areas of marketing. It grew into a corporate giant, amassing more than $11 billion in sales during 1988. It has done all this in manufacturing, not mining. But even if 2M is a more accurate name than 3M, the company keeps the mining portion of its name. It is a good reminder of the company's roots and the long battle it fought to be a successful, worldwide corporation.

3M developed cellophane tape, for which customers found many uses. The company adopted the brand name "Scotch" for many of its products.

Manufacturers will often adopt **brand names** to help customers tell the difference between their products and the products made by other manufacturers. The best brand names are those that are easy for customers to remember.

Marketing is the process of developing a product, determining how much it should cost, deciding how it should be sold, and making sure that people who want to buy the product can get it. One slogan describes marketing as "finding a need and filling it."

The Etch A Sketch®
Safety Scare

Ohio Art Company

Ohio Art faced a tough battle when its Etch A Sketch® was targeted by a consumer protection group.

WHEN THE OHIO ART COMPANY INTRO-duced the Etch A Sketch® in 1960, sales of the unique toy climbed rapidly. But about 10 years later, the company found its popular product under attack by consumer protection groups that said the toy was unsafe. They demanded that the Etch A Sketch® be banned from the store shelves and that those already sold be recalled.

While public-safety advocates have performed valuable service over the years in promoting auto safety, safe sleepwear for children, and proper disposal of hazardous wastes, they nearly ruined the reputation of the Ohio Art Company and the Etch A Sketch® with their false accusations. Sales of the drawing toy suffered during a highly publicized attack on the toy industry.

Picture frames featuring prints of "Cupid Awake" and "Cupid Asleep" were the first products manufactured by the Ohio Art Company.

The Ohio Art Company was founded in the early 1900s by a dentist who started a business to sell picture prints in metal frames. Henry Simon Winzeler had become fascinated by an oval mirror used by men trying on hats in a clothing store owned by his aunt and cousin. Winzeler thought the shape of the mirror's frame was so elegant that it would be a perfect display piece for mass-produced pictures.

In 1907 Winzeler borrowed $300 to order equipment for manufacturing oval picture frames. For nearly two years, while waiting for the equipment, he continued to work at his Archbold, Ohio, dentistry practice. Then he sold the practice and bought

A **manufacturing plant** is a building that contains equipment used in making products and is where products are made.

In general, an economic **depression** is a period when production and consumption of goods and services slow down. It is a time marked by unemployment and business failures, and people do not have much money to live on. During the 1930s, the United States suffered through a period called the **Great Depression**, during which the U.S. economy was paralyzed.

a grocery business to help finance the manufacturing plant. On October 6, 1908, Winzeler started the Ohio Art Company.

After expanding its facilities four times within three years, the Ohio Art Company relocated from Archbold to Bryan, Ohio, in 1912.

The company ventured into the toy business in 1917 when it bought the Erie Toy Plant from the C.E. Carter Company. The first toy was a metal windmill. It was followed by a climbing monkey on a string. The manufacturing plant was moved to Bryan, Ohio, the following year, and the first toy produced there was a metal tea set. Other early toys made by the company were a metal sand pail in 1923 and a circus train in 1929.

H.S. Winzeler retired from active management of the company in 1927, but continued to own the business. Three years later, he incorporated the business but kept 80 percent of the shares. His 15-year-old son, H.W. Winzeler, began working summers at the company in 1930. In 1933 H.W. Winzeler became a full-time employee of Ohio Art Company. The business continued to produce toys and prospered through the Great Depression.

Government restrictions limited the production of toys during World War II, and the Ohio Art Company switched to manufacturing products for the war effort. When the restrictions were lifted at the war's end in 1945, Ohio Art Company began making toys again. During the next decade, the company began manufacturing plastic toys like farm animals and tea sets.

While attending the German Toy Fair in 1959, H.W. Winzeler, who had become company president, first heard of a novel toy idea. It was a "magic screen" on which intricate designs could be etched and then erased. By the end of the year, Ohio Art had purchased the rights to manufacture the toy that eventually was named Etch A Sketch.®

Production of Etch A Sketch® began the following year. The product was a slim, bright red, plastic box with a window that resembled a television screen. Inside the window was a mixture of aluminum powder and plastic pellets. When the product was turned upside down and shaken, a silver coating of aluminum powder was left on the back of the glass. A pencil-like point inside the glass was operated by knobs on the top of the box. Wherever the point passed, it left a sharp line through the silver powder on the window.

H.W. Winzeler

The toy, helped by the company's first television advertising, was an instant success. It won seals of approval from both *Good Housekeeping* and *Parents* magazines and became popular with children. Within 10 years of the toy's introduction in the United States, more than a million of them were sold by a single retailer, Sears, Roebuck and Company.

In the late 1960s, however, consumer protection groups were focusing their attention on the toy-manufacturing industry. They listed several toys that

This 1960 advertisement was the first to introduce the Etch A Sketch® to the public.

they felt were dangerous, and Etch A Sketch® was one of the toys mentioned. The author of a book on potentially unsafe toys said that a child leaning on the Etch A Sketch® while drawing could break the glass window and get cut. A government-sponsored safety commission backed this up, claiming that 22 parents had filed lawsuits blaming the manufacturer for cuts.

There were accusations that the aluminum powder was poisonous and could cause burns. A national radio show went so far as to claim, wrongly, that it contained mercury, a toxic substance. At best, the consumer groups said the powder could get inside a cut and cause an infection.

Because of the accusations, sales of the Etch A Sketch® began to drop. Concerned parents hesitated to buy it for their children. As Ohio Art lost several million dollars in sales between 1969 and 1972, the future of the product looked less promising than it had before the false charges were made. Ohio Art fought to maintain its reputation by suing the people who had made false, damaging statements about the product.

Gradually, facts began to emerge from among the accusations. *Parents* magazine conducted a test to determine the danger of the aluminum powder. That test found no evidence that the powder would be harmful to children, even if they swallowed it.

Ohio Art Company then produced records showing that, of the millions of Etch A Sketch® units sold over a nine-year period, only 13 had produced complaints about broken glass. In a court demonstration, an Etch A Sketch® was dropped on a sidewalk more than 1,000 times without breaking. Researcher Marvin Kaye found that a randomly chosen Etch A Sketch® did not shatter even when he pounded it with a hammer.

Ohio Art eventually reclaimed the reputation of its product. It protected the toy against future allegations by equipping it with more safety features, such as a plastic sheet over the glass. But the toy's narrow brush with disaster shows that the business world has pitfalls lying in wait for even the most successful of products.

Most companies strive to develop an image as reliable providers of high-quality goods and services. When a company has a good **reputation**, it is likely to have many loyal customers. Ohio Art's reputation as a manufacturer of safe toys was damaged by accusations that children could be hurt by the Etch A Sketch.® By suing those who said the toy was unsafe, the company sought to prove in court that the Etch A Sketch® actually was safe.

1990 Etch A Sketch®—the package changed, but the product stayed the same.

It Almost Wasn't In the Cards

Hallmark

Joyce C. Hall

MANY FOUNDERS OF THE MOST SUC-
cessful companies have seen all their hopes and
dreams smashed. Rarely has catastrophe struck a
company as suddenly and with such force as it hit
Joyce Hall, who started Hallmark Cards, Inc. Just
when he had hope that his new company was beginning to dig out from under its mound of debts,
he received a phone call. By the time he hung up,
Hall was almost as poor as the most destitute tramp
in Kansas City.

Joyce Hall was born in 1891 in David City,
Nebraska. Because his mother admired a methodist
bishop named Isaac W. Joyce, Hall was given his
unusual first name, and he often used his initials,
J.C. His father left the family when the boy was
seven years old. With his mother, a semi-invalid,

unable to work, J.C. and his two older brothers were forced to find jobs.

Hall kept up his schoolwork and did odd jobs, such as selling perfume door-to-door, until the age of 11. Then he left David City to work part time in a bookstore that also sold picture postcards from Europe. Some of the cards were especially fancy works of art, full of frills and engravings, to be sent at Christmas and Valentine's Day.

Although people had sent valentines for centuries, the idea of sending artistic cards through the mail was a fairly new one. Formal Christmas cards are said to be a 19th-century British invention, started by a London government official who had put off sending his traditional Christmas notes until it was too late. In desperation he had sought out a printer who could produce a batch of formal greetings quickly. By the time Hall started his job at the bookstore, such cards had become popular items among those who could afford them.

Hall liked the idea of sending beautiful cards through the mail, and at the age of 18, he began selling them on his own to drugstores. Later that year, he moved his supply of picture postcards to Kansas City, where he started a mail-order business. His brother Rollie soon joined him, and the two of them gradually built up an inventory of postcards, stationery, and books. Joyce included a number of the expensive, imported Christmas and Valentine's Day cards in his stock.

A retail establishment, or store, that sells its goods through the postal system is called a **mail-order business**.

The products a manufacturer, company, or store has on hand are referred to as **inventory**.

J.C. Hall sold valentines shipped from other countries in the 1910s.

By 1912 Hall found that postcards were not selling as well as the previous year. To increase the business, he had to add new lines. Manufacturers had begun producing cheaper, poorer-quality postcards, and dime stores started selling them for 10 cents a dozen. Hall could see that greeting cards would have a better future than postcards. First, he added valentines. Many of them were sent in envelopes, which was an advantage over postcards because the message could remain private. Hall realized greeting cards could become a social custom. While many people had never taken postcards seriously, they would buy high-quality greeting cards.

By 1915, however, Hall still counted on Christmas and Valentine's Day cards for the bulk of his sales. He ordered a huge shipment of valentines, running up a debt of $17,000, and eagerly awaited the sales that would turn that debt into a profit. Instead, on the cold morning of January 11, Hall was awakened by a ringing telephone. The caller informed him that a fire had wiped out his Kansas City warehouse. Not only was the building gone, but the entire shipment of valentines had been destroyed. With only $9,000 of insurance to reimburse him, Hall was stuck in an almost impossible business situation. He had an enormous debt and had nothing with which to pay it off, let alone to buy new inventory.

That could have been the end of the Hall brothers' involvement in the greeting card business if a local banker had not taken a chance on them. By 10:00 A.M. the next morning, the company was operating again. Later that year, Hall Brothers bought a small engraving company and began printing its own designs. The year that started with a disaster ended on a high note for the young company.

Hall understood that social graces in the United States were far more casual than in the European countries where most of the postcards originated, and he steered his company's designs away from the embellished European look. Using a poem from Edgar Guest, "A Friend's Greeting," he had Christmas greetings engraved on cards with hand-painted poinsettias, a variety of Christmas flower.

These cards proved to be so popular that Hall kept his cards in production. He introduced cards for occasions such as birthdays and anniversaries.

Insurance is a way to cover the cost of unexpected losses —such as deaths, accidents, or fires—by dividing the cost among many individuals. An insured person doesn't have to pay the whole cost of the loss himself or herself—the insurance company pays it. A large group of people (the insured) pay a **premium** (a regular payment of money) to the insurance company. This provides the company with a large amount of money to cover any losses. Only a small percentage of the insured people will suffer the types of losses the insurance company will have to cover. Each insurance policy (the contract between the insured person and the company) specifies the maximum amount of money the company will pay in the event of a loss. Joyce Hall had more than $17,000 worth of property to protect, but the maximum amount of loss his insurance would cover was $9,000.

Many companies divide their market into **sales territories**. Each salesperson is given a specific territory, or geographic area, in which to sell the company's product. Usually, only one salesperson is assigned to each territory. By dividing its market into territories, a company can make sure all areas are represented, and that there is no competition between its salespeople for specific customers.

Hall Brothers also made get-well cards and sympathy cards.

The third of the Hall brothers, William, joined the company in 1920, and the three developed new sales territories in Nebraska, Oklahoma, and Kansas. As Hall Brothers expanded, Joyce Hall stressed quality and good taste. In 1923 the company's name was changed to the more elegant-sounding Hallmark. The company obtained the works of famous artists and writers, including Grandma Moses, Norman Rockwell, and British Prime Minister Winston Churchill, for its cards.

Norman Rockwell, visiting with a Hallmark employee in the 1950s, was one of several famous artists whose works were featured on Hallmark cards.

In 1951 Hallmark began sponsoring a series of television specials called the Hallmark Hall of Fame. Joyce Hall was not discouraged when the shows attracted few viewers. He liked having the company's name associated with quality productions of the classics.

"Good taste is good business," Joyce Hall was fond of saying. In order to ensure that Hallmark's fine taste never slipped, all new designs and verses had to be approved by a panel of judges. Joyce Hall was the final judge of designs and verses issued by Hallmark. From the time the company's first greeting card was sold in 1915 until Hall's retirement in 1966, no new card was issued without Joyce Hall's personal approval.

By the time of Joyce Hall's death in 1982, Hallmark greeting cards had become an important part of United States society. Hallmark produced more than eight million greeting cards each day. Yet, even a company as solid as Hallmark Cards, Inc. can look at its roots, then point to a list of bankruptcy notices and say, "That could have been us."

The Automaker's Crisis: Déjà Vu

Chrysler

Walter P. Chrysler

In THE LATE 1970s, THE CHRYSLER Corporation resembled the sinking ship *Titanic*. It had been sailing along smoothly, taking pride in its reputation as one of the top three manufacturers in the automobile industry. Suddenly, management mistakes, government regulations, an energy crisis, and a nationwide recession combined to rock the company to its core.

Chrysler cars were practically falling apart a year or two after customers bought them. Fewer and fewer people were buying Chrysler cars, and the company was sinking into debt. Even Chrysler management had no idea how desperate the company's situation was. They did know Chrysler was in trouble, though, and they recruited a man who had been one of their chief rivals to rescue them.

What would Walter Chrysler, the man who had founded the Chrysler Corporation more than 50 years earlier, have thought of the company's problems and its efforts to solve them? Probably, he would have thought he had a case of déjà vu—a feeling that he had seen the same thing before. When Lee Iacocca took over the presidency at Chrysler and brought the company back to profitability in the late 1970s and early 1980s, he was not breaking new ground. Iacocca was merely taking a page out of the old master's book. The crisis that nearly finished the Chrysler Corporation was remarkably similar to the one that had started it.

Lee Iacocca

Walter Chrysler was born in 1875 in Kansas. He bought his first car, a Locomobile, in 1908. At the time, he was working for the Union Pacific railroad. He spent $5,000 on the Locomobile, but instead of showing off his expensive new possession, Chrysler immediately took it apart. He had bought the machine to study it and figure out how it worked. After reassembling the automobile, Chrysler was ready to make cars his new life's work. He quit his $12,000-a-year job to work in the auto industry for half the salary.

Chrysler learned the automobile business so well that he worked his way into the presidency of General Motor's Buick division by 1917. Disagreements with the chairman over policy matters led to his resignation in 1920. By then the 45-year-old Chrysler had saved enough money to retire.

Walter Chrysler introduced the first Chrysler car in 1924.

Then, in 1924, the Maxwell Motor Company was failing. The company had survived the industry's chaotic early years and had established a fine reputation. But the Maxwell Motor Company soon found itself in financial trouble. Its creditors recruited a talented automobile manager from outside the company in the hope that he could save the company. The person they brought in was Walter Chrysler.

Almost as soon as he arrived at Maxwell, Chrysler pushed a new luxury car into production. The new model was ready for display at an important New York auto show, but the struggling company was denied space in the showroom. Rather than returning to Detroit, Chrysler rented the lobby of the Commodore Hotel, where many of the automobile executives gathered. The Chrysler display stole the show from the larger exhibit.

In 1925 Chrysler replaced the Maxwell Motor Company with the Chrysler Corporation. With the acquisition of the Dodge Brothers Manufacturing Company in 1928, and continued solid management, Chrysler Corporation captured 25 percent of the automobile market by Walter Chrysler's death in 1940. At the same time, it earned a reputation as an industry leader in design and engineering innovation.

During the 1950s and 1960s, quality-control problems eroded the company's image. Chrysler's sales fell far behind that of General Motors and Ford. Yet, going into the 1970s, there seemed to be no cause for alarm among Chrysler executives. Even if it was the smallest of the top three automakers, it was still one of the largest companies in the United States.

The storm hit suddenly in the early 1970s. Chrysler had dropped its emphasis on small cars, which generated little profit. Instead, the company spent $450 million dollars to restyle a more profitable line of large cars. But the Middle Eastern nations that supply most of the world's oil imposed an oil embargo on

The percentage of a company's product sales among all sales of the same product in a given market is called its **market share**. If Chrysler had 25 percent of the automobile market, that means one of every four cars sold was made by Chrysler.

About 60 percent of the world's known oil supply is in the Middle East and North Africa. In 1973 a number of the nations that own oil imposed an oil embargo on Western nations. An **embargo** is a ban on exports of certain products. (An **export** is a product that is sent to a foreign country to be sold.) When the Middle Eastern countries reduced sales of oil to the U.S., oil prices in the U.S. rose dramatically. Since gasoline is made from crude oil, gasoline prices also rose.

An **import** is a product that is brought in from a foreign country to be sold. Each country exports, or sends out, some products to be sold in other countries. Each country also imports, or brings in, products from other countries to be sold to its citizens.

A 1976 Volaré: Chrysler had to recall many of the cars because of mechanical defects.

the United States in 1973. Oil shortages led to gasoline shortages, which drove up the price of fuel. With gasoline prices so much higher, car buyers passed up large, gas-guzzling cars for small, fuel-efficient automobiles. Imported subcompacts, especially inexpensive Japanese models, hurt Chrysler's sales.

While Chrysler was reeling from this blow, more problems developed. Governments began to set standards for reducing pollution from automobiles. Laws required automobile manufacturers to make their products safer. The new laws were expensive for auto manufacturers, which had to pay for research and changes in production processes.

At the same time, interest rates climbed higher and higher. With income from sales lagging far behind expenses, Chrysler was forced to borrow money at these high rates to stay in business. The cost of paying off the debts rose along with the interest rates.

All of this would have been a severe challenge for the company under the best of conditions. But Chrysler had management problems as well. The company produced more cars than it could sell, and thousands of new cars were stored on outdoor lots in Michigan, where they became weather-beaten before they were sold. Chrysler was saddled with 360,000 unsold cars in 1975.

Chrysler's reputation for quality cars slipped as its new Volarés and Aspens suffered a rash of problems. The company recalled more than three million of the cars.

In 1978 Chrysler was in an almost hopeless situation. It needed new products to replace its unpopular ones. But new cars take years and millions of dollars to develop, and Chrysler had no money to spare. In a three-month period, the company had lost $159 million. Bankers were squeamish about lending more money to a company that seemed doomed to fail.

That year Chrysler went back to its roots. Just as the Maxwell Motor Company had done, Chrysler turned to a former rival to save the company. Lee Iacocca had just been fired as president of the Ford Motor Company, despite a solid career there. Iacocca knew Chrysler had problems when he accepted the job, but he later admitted that he hadn't known how bad the problems were until he had been on the job for several months.

Chrysler's financial experts had estimated the company would show a loss of $200 million during 1979. But when the early results came in, Chrysler had suffered a $207 million loss in three months. Chrysler needed to sell 2.3 million cars and trucks in 1979 to break even. The company did not sell even half that many. The shah, or king, of Iran (a country in the Middle East) was unexpectedly overthrown, and a decrease in oil production under the new leadership caused another energy crisis. At its worst point, Chrysler was down to its last $1 million—

enough to pay the bills that it normally accumulated in half an hour.

Iacocca realized that the company could be saved only by drastic action, and even he doubted if that would be enough. He targeted six methods of raising money: sales of assets, wage concessions, bank loans, government help, improved efficiency, and increased car sales. Each of them would have to come through in order for Chrysler to have a chance.

Selling assets was easy enough; Chrysler raised $300 million primarily by selling overseas property and companies, and its military tank operations. In 1980 the company's workers agreed to give up $462 million in fringe benefits (vacation time, insurance coverage, and other "extras" that are separate from wages), and management gave up $125 million in fringe benefits. Chrysler streamlined its production lines, reorganized the sales system, and developed a new line of front-wheel-drive, fuel-efficient cars.

Yet it seemed Chrysler was making no progress. In the second three-month period of 1980, it lost $536 million, more money than it had ever made in an entire year. Chrysler's market share had shrunk to less than 9 percent. Most analysts predicted failure. They said the best Chrysler could hope for was a merger with another company.

Iacocca pleaded with the United States government to step in and help. He pointed out that a Chrysler failure could cost the country up to $16 billion from the loss of 100,000 jobs. Chrysler did

An **asset** is something of value that can be sold for money.

A **merger** is a union of two or more companies in which one company buys another. In recent years, mergers (sometimes called takeovers) have become common.

not want a government bailout, he said. All it needed was for the government to guarantee the banks that, if Chrysler should fail, the government would pay back the loans that the corporation needed in order to regain its profitability. After heated debates, in which many public officials argued against government involvement in private business, the loan guarantees were given.

Had the government simply given Chrysler money to pay off its debts, the action would have been called a **bailout.** As it was, government only guaranteed banks that it would pay off loans made to Chrysler if the company failed to repay them.

Television commercials featuring Iacocca helped the company's return to profitability.

The Reliant, one of the K-cars, turned out to be a great success for the company—once Chrysler made them affordable for the average customer.

Next, Iacocca had to regain the public's trust. With his tough, honest talk, Iacocca proved to be an ideal spokesperson for Chrysler commercials. He admitted Chrysler's past mistakes and simply told the public that Chrysler would back its new K-cars 100 percent. All he asked was for people to take a look.

Chrysler knew that if the K-cars did not sell well, the company was doomed, and early 1981 sales were disappointing. Analyzing the problem quickly, the company discovered there were too many options—cassette players, air conditioning, special wheels, and power windows—included with the cars. The added options raised the sticker price above what many people could afford to pay. After the company took out many of the options, sales picked up.

In 1982 Chrysler showed no financial loss for the year. In 1983 the corporation not only made money, it chalked up a record profit. Government accountants who had thought the federal government would be paying back the $1.2 billion Chrysler borrowed were surprised when Chrysler repaid the loans seven years early.

Chrysler had survived its greatest crisis, and Lee Iacocca was showered with praise for the miraculous turnaround. Walter Chrysler probably would not have been as awed as most observers, however. The styles and the sales figures may have changed over the years, but the automobile business was still the same. Rescuing a car company was all part of a day's work for an auto executive.

For Further Reading...

Bryant, K.L., Jr. and Dethloff, H.C. *A History of American Business*. Prentice-Hall Inc., 1983.

Clary, D.C. *Great American Brands*. Fairchild Books, 1981.

Fucini, J.J. and Fucini, S. *Entrepreneurs: The Men and Women Behind Famous Brand Names*. G.K. Hall, 1985.

Livesay, H.C. *American Made: Men Who Shaped the American Economy*. Little, Brown & Company, 1980.

Moskowitz, M., Katz, M. and Levering, R., eds. *Everybody's Business*. Harper and Row, 1980.

Sobel, R. and Sicilia, D.B. *The Entrepreneurs: An American Adventure*. Houghton Mifflin Company, 1986.

Thompson, J. *The Very Rich Book*. William Morrow & Company, 1981.

Vare, E. and Ptacek, G. *Mothers of Invention: From the Bra to the Bomb: Forgotten Women and Their Unforgettable Ideas*. William Morrow & Company, 1988.

INDEX

Words in **boldface** are defined in the text.

A

A. Bushnell & Company, 34
advertising, definition of, 31
Anchor Brand canned goods, 27
Aspen (car), 71
asset, definition of, 73
Astor Fur Company, 14
Augsbury & Moore Corner Store, 34, 35

B

bailout, definition of, 74
bankruptcy, definition of, 16
board of directors, definition of, 50
Bovee, William, 19-20
boycott, definition of, 20
brand names, definition of, 54

C

C.E. Carter Company, 57
Case School of Applied Sciences, 42, 46
Chrysler, Walter P., 67-70, 75
Chrysler Corporation, 7, 8, 67-75
Churchill, Winston, 65
Columbian Exposition, 30
Columbus, Christopher, 30
Commodore Hotel, 70
competition, definition of, 42
contract, definition of, 20
controlling interest, definition of, 16
credit, definition of, 15
creditor, definition of, 15
Creighton, Jennie, 34

D

debt, definition of, 16
demand, definition of, 19
depression, definition of, 57
development, *see* research and development
distribution, definition of, 20
distributor, definition of, 20
Dodge Brothers Manufacturing Company, 70
Dow, Herbert Henry, 41-48
Dow Chemical Company, 8, 41-48
Dow Process Company, 46
Du Pont, Eleuthère Irénée, 11-16
Du Pont, Pierre, 12-13
Du Pont, Pierre (Pete), 11
Du Pont Company, 7, 8, 11-16

E

E.I. du Pont de Nemours & Co., *see* Du Pont Company
embargo, definition of, 70
equity, definition of, 28
Erie Toy Plant, 57
Etch A Sketch® 55-60
expansion, definition of, 23
export, definition of, 71

F

F & J Heinz Company, 30
F.W. Woolworth Co., 7, 8, 33-40
Folger, James, 17-23

Folger, Samuel, 17-18
Folger's, 8, 17-23
Ford Motor Company, 70, 72
French Revolution, 12

G

General Motors, 68, 70
Good Housekeeping magazine, 58
Grandma Moses, 65
Great Depression, definition of, 57
Griswold, Tom, 47-48
Grumman, Leroy, 9
Grumman Corporation, 9

H

H.J. Heinz Company, 7, 8, 25-32
Hall, Joyce C., 61-66
Hall, Rollie, 62
Hall, William, 65
Hall Brothers, 64-65
Hallmark Cards, Inc., 7, 9, 61-66
Heinz, Frank, 29
Heinz, Henry John, 25-32
Heinz, John, 29
Heinz, Noble & Company, 27-28
Helman, B.E., 45

I

Iacocca, Lee, 68, 72-75
import, definition of, 71
insurance, definition of, 64
inventory, definition of, 62
investor, definition of, 13

J

J.A. Folger & Co., 22
Jefferson, Thomas, 12, 14
Joyce, Isaac W., 61

K

Kaye, Marvin, 60
K-cars, 75
King Louis XVI, 12

L

Locomobile, 68

M

Macy, Rowland Hussey, 7-8
Macy's department store, 7-8
mail-order business, definition of, 62
manufacturing, definition of, 20
manufacturing plant, definition of, 57
Marden & Folger, 20-21
market, definition of, 19
marketing, definition of, 54
market share, definition of, 70
Maxwell Motor Company, 68-70, 72
McKnight, Virginia, 52
McKnight, William, 52-53
merger, definition of, 73
Midland Chemical Company, 44, 46
Minnesota Mining and Manufacturing,
    9, 49-54
Moore, William, 35-36
Moore & Smith's Corner Store, 35

N

Noble, E.J., 27
Noble, L.C., 27

O

Ober, Edgar, 50-51
Ohio Art Company, 9, 55-60
Ordway, Lucius, 50-51

P

packaging, definition of, 26
Parents magazine, 58, 60
patent, definition of, 45
Pioneer Steam Coffee and Spice Mills, 19-20
premium (payment), definition of, 64
price wars, definition of, 42
production, definition of, 20
profit, definition of, 15
promotion, definition of, 31

Q

quality control, definition of, 53

R

Reliant (car), *see* K-cars
reputation, definition of, 60
research and development, definition of, 43
Rockwell, Norman, 65

S

sales territories, definition of, 65
Schilling spices, 23
stockholders, definition of, 50
stocks, definition of, 16
supply, definition of, 19

T

3M, *see* Minnesota Mining and Manufacturing
Treaty of Paris (1783), 12

U

under-capitalized, definition of, 30
Union Pacific railroad, 68

V

Volaré (car), 71

W

War of 1812, 15
Winzeler, H.W., 57-58
Winzeler, Henry Simon, 56-57
Woolworth, Frank Winfield, 33-40
Woolworth Corporation, *see* F.W. Woolworth Co.
World War II, 57

Y

Young, Sarah (Sallie) Sloan, 27

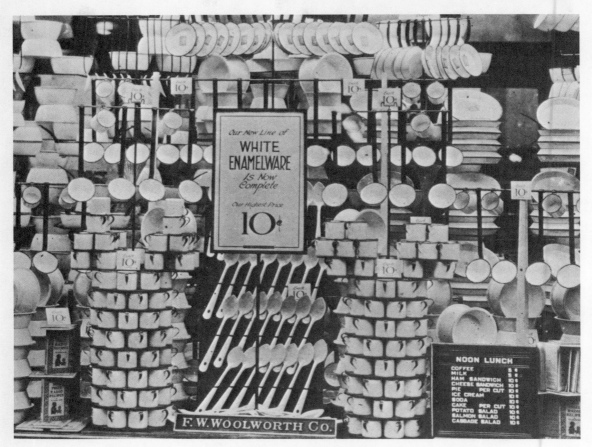

Woolworth's window displays drew customers into the stores.

ACKNOWLEDGEMENTS

The photographs and illustrations in this book are reproduced through the courtesy of: pp. 1, 49, 51, 52, 53, 54, 3M; pp. 2, 24, 27, 29, 30, 31, 32, H.J. Heinz Company; pp. 6, 8, The Macy Archives; p. 9, Grumman Corporation; pp. 10, 12, 14, 15, 16, Du Pont Company; pp. 17, 19, 21, 22, The Procter & Gamble Company; pp. 35, 37, 38, 40, 80, Woolworth Corporation; pp. 41, 43, 44, 48, The Dow Chemical Company; pp. 55, 56, 58, 59, 60, The Ohio Art Company; pp. 61, 63, 65, 66, Hallmark Corporate Archives, Hallmark Cards, Inc.; pp. 67, 68, 69, 71, 74, 75, Chrysler Corporation.

Cover illustration by Stephen Clement.